To Mum & Grandpa, Abby & Popper—great babysitters all.
And always, to my Committee, with love.
—H. M.

In loving memory of my grandmother, Susan Z. Brown
—L. R.

What to Expect
When the
Babysitter Comes

Heidi Murkoff
Illustrated by Laura Rader

HarperFestival®
A Division of HarperCollinsPublishers

A Word to Parents

Whether you're heading out for a night of romance, an afternoon of recreation, or a day of work, there will be plenty of times when you'll need to (or want to) leave home without children. Enter: the babysitter.

If this is the first time ever a babysitter is coming to your home, or if it's the first time a new babysitter is coming (particularly if she's taking the place of a favorite), preparation will help ease your child's anxieties about the unknown.

What to Expect When the Babysitter Comes is a good place to begin that preparation. It will answer many of the questions your child may have about babysitters—what they're for, what they're like, what they do—as well as concerns about how the day or night will be different (and the same) without Mommy and Daddy around. It will also help your child understand (and, hopefully, begin to appreciate) why mommies and daddies need and want occasional or regular kid-free time. It's a subtle subtext but an important message: Mommies and daddies love their children but still reserve time that's just for themselves.

In reading this book you'll see there are many ideas for activities to acclimate your child to the idea of having a babysitter. Many of these are role-playing activities that turn your child into the babysitter. Playing babysitter before the babysitter comes will help your child feel more comfortable with this new experience—just as playing dentist before a trip to the dentist or playing barbershop before a haircut would. Other activities put your child in charge of prepping

the babysitter for her new job—making lists with you of favorite foods, toys, and bedtime rituals, or taking her for a tour of your home. These activities will help your child feel more in control of a situation he or she might otherwise feel powerless in; this control can also help increase comfort. (Though I refer to the babysitter as "she" throughout the book, if your child will be having a male babysitter, you can change "she" to "he" as you read.)

Preparation shouldn't end with reading this book, though. It will also help to invite the babysitter to come a little early, so both she and your child can get acquainted while you're still around. When it's time to leave, however, do so without drama or delay—and with a short, sweet, and upbeat good-bye ritual. Children often won't "give in" to the idea of having a babysitter (and having Mommy and Daddy leave) until there's no other option. Only after you leave can babysitter and child really get to know each other. Only then can the babysitting begin.

You'll notice that I have help explaining to your child what to expect when the babysitter comes. Because learning should be fun, too, I've created Angus, a lovable dog who provides answers to questions about growing up. Angus serves as a best friend and confidante throughout all of the What to Expect Kids™ books. He's a "transitional object" who will hold your child's hand as he or she faces new—and sometimes challenging—experiences.

For many more tips on choosing and using childcare, as well as preparing your child for a babysitter, read *What to Expect the Toddler Years*.

Wishing you lots of luck when the babysitter comes (and don't forget to enjoy your time away . . .)!

Come on! Let's go meet the babysitter.

Angus

Just Ask Angus

Hello! My name is Angus. Some people call me the Answer Dog, because I like to answer all kinds of questions about growing up. It's good to ask questions because what you know, helps you grow!

So, I hear you're going to have a babysitter. Maybe it's the first time you're having a babysitter, or maybe it's the first time you're meeting a new babysitter. Either way, that sounds like fun!

Did you know that all different kinds of people can be babysitters? An aunt or grandpa, an older boy or girl, a neighbor, or even a teacher. But all babysitters have one thing in common—they like children a lot!

Even if you've had a babysitter before, I bet you still have a lot of questions about what happens when a babysitter comes to your house. I'm here to help—just ask me!

Are you ready to find out what to expect when the babysitter comes and what you can do to help? Then let's get started! Follow me. . . .

Your friend,

Angus

P.S. I've put a little game or idea to think about on the bottom of every page. Look for my paw print, and you'll find it! Have fun!

What's a babysitter?

A babysitter is someone who comes to your house to take care of you when Mommy and Daddy aren't home. A babysitter is your own special "company"—a visitor who comes to spend time with you and to play with you. Your babysitter may be a woman or a man, or an older girl or a boy. Your babysitter can be someone you know a little, like a neighbor, or someone you know a lot, like a grandma or an aunt or uncle or a teacher from your school. Or she may be someone you are meeting for the very first time. And you know what that means? That you'll be getting to know a brand-new friend!

You can pretend to be a babysitter who comes to take care of a child in your house. The child can be a stuffed animal or doll, or it can even be your mommy or daddy. It's especially fun to play this game when your babysitter comes!

You can play this game with your babysitter.

Why do I have to have a babysitter?

Sometimes Mommy and Daddy need to go out without you. Maybe they're going to work or school, or out to dinner, or to their friends' house (mommies and daddies have friends, just like you). Even though you're pretty big, you still need someone to stay with you and help take care of you when Mommy and Daddy aren't home. All children do. That's why Mommy and Daddy ask your babysitter to come over.

Pretend you're babysitting again. Where are the child's parents going while you babysit?

They might go out to dinner.

Why can't I just go with Mommy and Daddy?

There are plenty of things your mommy and daddy like to do with you, like go to the playground, draw pictures, and bake cookies. But there are other things that your mommy and daddy like to do by themselves or need to do by themselves. Those are usually grown-up things at grown-up places. I bet you'll have more fun at home with your babysitter. And when Mommy and Daddy come home or when you see them in the morning, they can tell you all about where they were and what they did!

Can you name some other fun things that Mommy and Daddy do with you?

I love to go to the beach, don't you?

When will Mommy and Daddy go?

Mommy and Daddy won't go until your babysitter comes to stay with you. If it's the first time your babysitter is taking care of you, your mommy and daddy will help you get to know each other. They will tell the babysitter what she'll need to know while they're away, like when your bedtime is. You can be a big help by showing your babysitter where your room is, what your favorite toys are, and where to find your special towel after your bath. Then, when Mommy and Daddy are ready, it will be time for them to leave. Maybe you can wave to them from the door or the window!

A song or rhyme always makes it easier to say good-bye. You can make up your own with Mommy and Daddy, or you can say my favorite: "See you later, alligator . . . after a while, crocodile!"

What will I do when Mommy and Daddy are gone?

You can put together puzzles. You can pretend to be a firefighter. You can play teddy bear hospital. You can race cars and trucks. You can look at books and listen to music. You can play dress up, have a tea party, draw or color, take a nap or a bath, maybe even go to the park if it's daytime and the weather's nice. In fact, you can do all of the same fun things you do when Mommy and Daddy are home. And remember, your babysitter spends lots of time playing with children, so she may know lots of other fun things to do.

What are some things you like to do? Help Mommy or Daddy make a list of these fun things to give to your babysitter.

What if I get hungry when the babysitter comes?

Your babysitter can make you meals and snacks when you're hungry and give you something to drink when you're thirsty. To make sure she knows what your favorite foods and drinks are, and what cups and plates you like to use, help your mommy or daddy make a list. They can print the words, and you can draw pictures. Then you can give the list to your babysitter when she comes so she'll know just what you like to eat and drink.

I like fruit for snack, too!

Pretend you're the babysitter again. Does the child you're taking care of have a favorite snack and a favorite drink? What are they?

What if I have to go to the potty? What if I need my shoes tied?

Your babysitter can do just about everything a mommy or daddy can do. She can help you go to the potty or change your diaper. She can tie your shoes or put your teddy bear's jacket on. She can wash the jelly off your face or clean up a spill. She can kiss a boo-boo, if you have one, and put on a fresh Band-Aid. And when you need a hug, she can give you one of those, too. Don't forget to hug back!

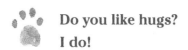

**Do you like hugs?
I do!**

Do babysitters have children like me?

Some babysitters have little children just like you. Some babysitters have grown-up children and little grandchildren. Some babysitters don't have any children at all. But all babysitters like children, all babysitters like to play with children, and all babysitters like to take care of children—and that's why they like to babysit so much!

Babysitting is a good job for people who like children. Can you think of other good jobs for people who like children?

Teachers like children, too.

Will the babysitter put me to bed?

Sometimes, when Mommy and Daddy won't be home until after bedtime, your babysitter will put you to bed. Before she comes, help Mommy or Daddy make a list of all the bedtime things you like to do, so your babysitter will know when your bedtime is and the right way to put you to bed. On the list you can tell her if you like bubbles in your bath, what kind of snack you like to eat, where your toothbrush is, what your favorite bedtime stories are, and which teddy bear you like to be tucked in with. Then when you wake up in the morning, you can tell Mommy and Daddy all the fun things you and your babysitter did together!

Maybe she'd like to hear your favorite story.

Good Night, Angus

Angus

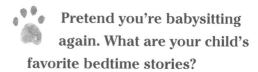

Pretend you're babysitting again. What are your child's favorite bedtime stories?

When will Mommy and Daddy come back?

Most times Mommy and Daddy will go out for a few hours, but sometimes they may need to be away for a few days or a whole week. Ask your mommy or daddy to tell you or show you on the clock or the calendar when they will be back. Sometimes you'll already be asleep when they come home, and you'll see them when you wake up in the morning. Sometimes you'll still be awake. But one thing you can be sure of: Mommy and Daddy will always, always come home.

That's special! Mommy and Daddy will love it!

Next time Mommy and Daddy go out, make a special picture for them while they're gone. Leave it as a present they can see when they come home. I bet they'll love it!